Rhyming Wonders

Edited By Jenni Harrison

First published in Great Britain in 2020 by:

Young Writers
Remus House
Coltsfoot Drive
Peterborough
PE2 9BF
Telephone: 01733 890066
Website: www.youngwriters.co.uk

Printed and bound in the UK by BookPrintingUK
Website: www.bookprintinguk.com
YB0431G

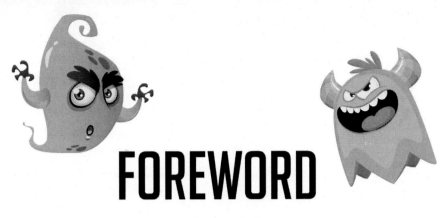

FOREWORD

Hello Reader!

For our latest poetry competition we sent out funky and vibrant worksheets for primary school pupils to fill in and create their very own poem about fiendish fiends and crazy creatures. I got to read them and guess what? They were **roarsome**!

The pupils were able to read our example poems and use the fun-filled free resources to help bring their imaginations to life, and the result is pages **oozing** with exciting poetic tales. From friendly monsters to mean monsters, from bumps in the night to **rip-roaring** adventures, these pupils have excelled themselves, and now have the joy of seeing their work in print!

Here at Young Writers we love nothing more than poetry and creativity. We aim to encourage children to put pen to paper to inspire a love of the written word and explore their own unique worlds of creativity. We'd like to congratulate all of the aspiring authors that have created this book of **monstrous mayhem** and we know that these poems will be enjoyed for years to come. So, dive on in and submerge yourself in all things furry and fearsome (and perhaps check under the bed!).

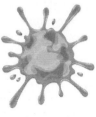

CONTENTS

Isabelle Kendall (9)   64
Evie Stratford Burden (10)   65
Seth Piper (11)   66
Aiden Austin (8)   67
Harvey Dowling (9)   68
Emily Silk (9)   69
Charlie Carver (10)   70
Brandon-Lee Stuart Gray (9)   71

Kirtlington CE Primary School, Kirtlington

Daisy Johnson (8)   72
Char Darke (8)   74
Will Langrish (9)   75
Isabelle Houselander (9)   76
Holly Cole (9)   77
Lola Jenkins (10)   78
Aria Miller (9)   79
Ayla Mansell (9)   80
Seth Flood (9)   81
Lucy Charlesworth (9)   82
Zach Bradney (9)   83
Alex Grebot (9)   84
Sam Bartlett (8)   85
Ernie Emmerson (8)   86
Dotty Dartnell (8)   87
James Allison (8)   88
Finley Mundy (9)   89
Arthur Dartnall (10)   90

Marsh Lane Primary School, Marsh Lane

Saxony-Brook Betts (10)   91
Mya Grace Jans (10)   92
Joseph Hobson (10)   94
Natalie Graham (10)   96
Ruby May (11)   97
Joshua Hebb (10)   98
Bailey Harrison Williams (10)   99
Dylan Millington (10)   100
Lily-Mae Coulson (10)   101
Zach Burdett (10)   102

Thomas George Evison (10)   103
Alfie Marshall (10)   104
Micah Burlaga (10)   105

Saints & Scholars Integrated Primary School, Armagh

Holly Horner (10)   106
Sophie Bradley (9)   108
Odette O'Donnell (9)   110
Hera Araja (9)   112
Kate Grimley (9)   113
Beth Erin Patrick (9)   114
Aalia Donnelly (11)   115
Mia Ewart (10)   116
Oliver (9)   117
Aimee Murray (9)   118
Nathaniel Faulkner (10)   119
Aine McCann-Wilson (9)   120

St Helens PACE PRU, Parr

Christopher Shaw (7)   121
Adrian Tomcik (7)   122
Charlie Unsworth (8)   123
Leon Jones (6)   124
Joseph Anglesey-Mahoney (7)   125

St John Of Jerusalem CE Primary School, Hackney

Anna Wilson (9)   126
Nathan Minganu (9)   128
Edward Skrine (10)   129
Matthew Erhunnwunsee (9)   130
Nathan Precilla (9)   131
Paige Violet Blaxill (10)   132
Chukwudi Favour Emmanuel-Echerenwa (9)   133
Harley Holdip Henry (9)   134

St Patrick's Primary School, Kilsyth

Patrick Phillips (10)	135
Ellie Morrison (10)	136
Zara Valentine Higney (9)	137
Aiden Gall (10)	138
Dolina Brannan (9)	139
John Jack Dynan (10)	140
Taylor David Burns (10)	141
Sophie Boyle (10)	142
Lewis Campbell (9)	143
Kyle Johnston (9)	144
Thomas Neil (9)	145

The Learning Zone, Longfleet Road

Ella-Louise Whiteley (8)	146
Alex Carlos (10)	147
Alice Lloyd (6)	148

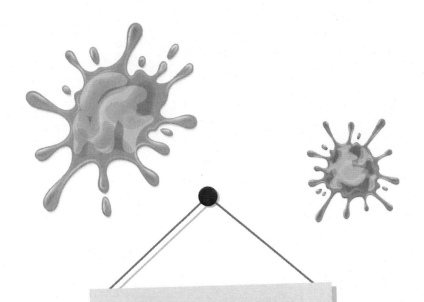

THE POEMS

I'm Friends With A Monster

I'm friends with a monster, his name is Jeffrey
Growl.
He sometimes has a temper, but he hardly ever
frowns.
His favourite food is broccoli, which I never
understand.
And he loves to play on my Xbox and watch Alice
in Wonderland.
What is funny about him, is his teeny-tiny horns.
'Cause he makes them go 'toot, toot'
Like a trumpet kind of noise.
His little brother, Jimmy, though is a tiny, little
devil.
He runs around breaking things and pooping on
the table.
But he is a brilliant gamer. Yes, he is.
Every time he plays a game he beats every level.
Oh my! Oh my! I think his brother's jealous!
So, yes, I'm friends with a monster.
And I hope you meet them too!

Sam Haraben (10)

Billinge St Aidan's CE Primary School, Billinge

Monstrous Garry

My big and scary monster
Eats children for a treat.
He bounces all around the place.
Stomping with his hairy feet.

He frightens all the children,
They scream and run away.
Poor old monster,
All he wants to do is play.

He searches all around the town
Looking for a friend.
Up hills, and down roads,
And even round the bend.

He finally finds some friends,
Playing and having fun.
They ask if he would like to play
And a whole new friendship has begun.

The children love their monster friend.
Their days are full of laughter.

The monster is not lonely now.
Happily ever after.

Llorienna Raywood (9)
Billinge St Aidan's CE Primary School, Billinge

The Musty Monster

Hairy and furry
And short and scary.
The monster is coming tonight
Don't raise an eye, he will give you a fright.
So as he passes by you best watch the time
As you carry on reading this spooky rhyme.
Dark in the park
You won't see a spark.
So don't dare to cry
Or say goodbye.
When you get home
Book a ticket to Rome.
You'll be safer there,
Than you would anywhere.

Anthony John Dockerty (10)
Billinge St Aidan's CE Primary School, Billinge

Brutal Bob

Bob is spiky.
When people see him they say, crikey!
Bob is big-mouthed, so he can eat food.
He has no friends and people think he's crude.
Bob is very, very spotty.
He says to himself, "I am very dotty."
He lives like an animal in the Amazon Forest.
He's naughty and is never at his sorriest.
His belly rumbles like thunder.
You can find him in a cave which is under.

Sam Shipley (9)
Billinge St Aidan's CE Primary School, Billinge

Powerful Eleven

I can see a mean girl
What should I do?
Should I use my powers
Or should I let them be mean?
Should I get Mikey
Or should I let him be?
Children, keep away,
Don't be bullied.
Just stay under your covers
And keep away.
Don't get out,
Just keep away.
My friends are kind.
Come and meet them,
They won't hurt you.
Come out and play with me.

Olivia Darbyshire (10)
Billinge St Aidan's CE Primary School, Billinge

The Woodshed

Don't go into the woodshed,
Don't go in at all!
Do you want to see the light of day?
Do you want to breathe again?
Don't go into the woodshed,
Don't go in at all.
There is a mechanical monster
Lurking all around.
I barely got out alive!
I almost didn't make it!
So I'm telling you...
DON'T GO INTO THE WOODSHED!
DON'T GO IN AT ALL!

Ethan Roughley (9)
Billinge St Aidan's CE Primary School, Billinge

Monster's Day Out!

The fear of the night creeps through my bed.
Creeping, keeping me awake.
Flosso is coming for a feast
On Dad's delicious chocolate dinner.
Come with me, we can go to the park
And have ice cream all day.
We will go tomorrow
And have a feast at the feast.
We have jelly, chocolate, sandwiches and cakes.
I love you monster,
You're perfect.

Ella Nicholson (9)
Billinge St Aidan's CE Primary School, Billinge

What Is That Noise?

What was that noise?
It sounded loud.
What was that noise?
It formed a black cloud.

I saw a shadow.
It was very big.
I saw a shadow.
It sounded like a pig.

I looked through the door.
I saw a figure.
I looked through the door.
It just got bigger.

I opened my door...
It was just my mum.

Owen Nicholas Walker (10)

Billinge St Aidan's CE Primary School, Billinge

Monster Under The Bed

There is a scary, sticky, creepy monster under my bed.

I can hear his claw going across my bed.

The monster is here and he likes to eat children, but obviously me.

When we're all asleep he eats my food, but I get the blame.

I've seen him once. He is fluffy and has three eyes and a spiky belly.

Does anyone know what this thing is?

Charlie Cosgrove (9)

Billinge St Aidan's CE Primary School, Billinge

Swirly Seed

I can feel spikes from under my bed.
I can hear a hairy back rubbing against my door.
When I go downstairs I step in slime.
As I turn the light off, I see a spooky shadow.
I went to my yummy snacks
And they were all eaten.
I woke up last night
And I saw a slimy, swirly, hairy monster peeking
at me.
Who is he?

Ruby Gedman-Cunliffe (9)
Billinge St Aidan's CE Primary School, Billinge

Monty The Monster

Monty the monster is a creepy-crawly
And he likes a bedtime story.
Then when he wakes
He likes to eat cakes.
Next, he says, "I'm going to the park,
For a play with the bark."
When Monty the monster is finished at the park
He goes for a walk in the dark to the pub
Where he eats some wormy grub.

Chloe Kewley (9)
Billinge St Aidan's CE Primary School, Billinge

The Bed Monster

I am a monster, lost in LA.
I will gobble you up
If you do not sleep.
You can't kill me!
And you go. Bye!
To my bottomless pit,
You can't run or hide.
So stay in bed tonight.
Or you will have a fright.
Come to me
And you will disappear.
I can now eat your city
In one go. Bye-bye!

Liam Dean Buckley (9)

Billinge St Aidan's CE Primary School, Billinge

Prickly Poem

Prickly the monster is coming inside.
There's nowhere to run, and there's nowhere to hide.
You better get out before he spikes you with his head,
And if you leave this town, there are lots of places to dread.
Prickly, who's scary, is coming for you
To eat you and munch you like a ferocious tiger too.

Madeline Haggerty (9)
Billinge St Aidan's CE Primary School, Billinge

Millie The Monster

Big, hairy and searching for food.
Is she in a good mood?
Kind and cuddly.
Nice and snuggly.
Half horse.
Very nice.
But what does she eat?
What's her favourite treat?
I think it is food, any kind.
Wind her up
And she will gobble you up.
So don't end up on her plate!

Abigail Heaton (9)
Billinge St Aidan's CE Primary School, Billinge

Milo On The Move

He doesn't like to stay at home.
On holiday he likes to roam.
But when it starts to thunder and rain,
Back home he likes to go again.
Then suddenly behind my back door
I hear a loud and monstrous roar!
I peek and then I see an eye,
And then I shout, "Oh my!"

Ava Tushingham (10)
Billinge St Aidan's CE Primary School, Billinge

The Hungry Monster

There is a monster,
His name is Gary.
In the night he pats his belly.
When you wake up, all your food is gone.
You hear a rumble.
It could be him?
He walks around, searching for food.
His favourite snack is a cat.
He is very friendly.
Could you be his friend?

Ethan Colley (9)
Billinge St Aidan's CE Primary School, Billinge

Powerful Monsters

They will give you a fright
Or it will hug you too tight.
This powerful monster is as friendly as a puppy.
As flexible as a piece of paper.
As powerful as a machine.
Watch out for this monster, it may give you a bite.
But if you are careful, it will give you some rights.

Lilly Brown (9)
Billinge St Aidan's CE Primary School, Billinge

Sleep Tight

Cuddle, cuddle, cuddle me.
It will bring you lots of glee.
I love hugs but beware
If I snooze you're stuck there!
Snoring, snoring, under a tree,
That is where you'll find me!
I'm as fluffy as can be,
Cuddle me and you will see.

Megan Grace Codling (9)
Billinge St Aidan's CE Primary School, Billinge

Naughty Ned!

I sometimes get in trouble.
I like to try to be kind.
I'm spotty, scary and hairy
But I don't really shine.
I would love to be a friend
And be kind and caring too.
It would mean the world to me
And mean the world to you too!

Emily Ross (9)
Billinge St Aidan's CE Primary School, Billinge

The Monster In My Room!

Slimie Slimie, that's me.
I shoot it at you. Ha!
I stick to the wall
I do not fall
Down, I jump down
And scare you
Do not flee
It's me
My teeth are razors.
You will scream, flee,
When you do, you will see me.

Lindsey Jo Cunliffe (10)
Billinge St Aidan's CE Primary School, Billinge

One Friendly Monster

It wears a diamond dress,
This won't get you distress.
Her cosmic magic
Really is not tragic.
She is really kind,
Keep all this in mind.
You cannot trick her,
She has lots of fur!
Luna sparkles here,
Never ever fear!

Bea Hill (9)
Billinge St Aidan's CE Primary School, Billinge

The Monster In The Mansion

Sparkly, sparkly, sparkly. That is me.
I'm as pretty as can be, look at me
And you will see. Cuddle me
And you'll have tea,
But just make sure it's with me.

Grace Morris (9)
Billinge St Aidan's CE Primary School, Billinge

Slug Snot

Slimy slugs, gooey goo,
The monster Slug Snot is coming for you.
Nowhere to hide, nowhere to run.
Good luck. Hope you have lots of fun.
Could you be the next victim?

Mya Ellenthorpe (9)
Billinge St Aidan's CE Primary School, Billinge

Rolls Like A Wheel

He rolls like a wheel
Through the city.
His name is Dreg.
He eats cats.
He is the spotty, funny monster.

Elijah Colley (9)
Billinge St Aidan's CE Primary School, Billinge

Jack The New York Monster

Jack is a terrifying monster.
He starts as a lizard
Finding food.
But in the woods
You know that you're lost.
So the military test the area
Where Jack lives
And he started to be
A giant monster
That moved to a new area.

So he went to live in New York.
In the dark of night,
He was the size of the Burj Khalifa
New York was doomed
They evacuated
Leaving everything behind.
Later a human kills Jack
By slaying the monster
And takes back New York.

Ethan Robert Carrick (9)
Croft Community School, Annfield Plain

The Demon Boy

One blink makes the people cry,
Demon Boy is running by.
With red eyes glowing like the sun in the sky
And sharp teeth to eat a human pie!
Demon Boy is as big as a car, mean as a witch.
His frightful claws will make you twitch!

Jake Gascoinge (11)
Croft Community School, Annfield Plain

Way to Go Nikki!

My dinosaur is nutty
And fluffy, and soft.
My dinosaur is a T-rex.
Nikki is her name.
She's cute and fluffy
And soft and green.

Ellie Softley (9)
Croft Community School, Annfield Plain

Rotten Apple

In the dark of night
Rotten Apple was sloping
To the ground.
He was looking for his lunch.
Before the Grinch ate his lunch.

Abbey Louise Ware (9)
Croft Community School, Annfield Plain

Wibbly Wonders

When you're sat in bed
With your ted,
Wibbles is ready to fill your head
With lovely things from her land,
Like her favourite types of sand.
On the huge monster beach
She found a leech.
Her monster hugs are sticky like glue,
Will she ever hug you?
I held her hand and squeezed it tight
As we stumbled out into the night.
She showed me all her monster friends
But I was sad it was coming to an end.
We laughed and played all night long
Until I heard a wibbly song.
After I had said goodbye
She was rising and rising till she started to fly.
Suddenly I woke and heard the thunder,
I was so lost in wonder.

I looked out the window
And saw the sun gleam,
Was it all just a dream?

Emily Matthews (9)
Emsworth Primary School, Emsworth

Rumble Tumble Fungle!

Your dark, deep drain has a despicable visitor inside.
The one and only Rumble Tumble Fungle, the monster!

As he hunts for delicious insects he throws up fungal infections to keep him entertained.

He hopes that every human in a bathroom is very ill and that they are as evil as Rumble Tumble Fungle.

If a human enters Rumble Tumble Fungle's messy territory he is determined to make him sick.

Rumble Tumble Fungle is always starving.
If he sees anything edible he will devour it in seconds.

Rumble Tumble Fungle's favourite part of the day is sleeping.
Bam! He is fast asleep and he loves eating,
he loves Monster Munch!

Anika Avasthi (9)
Emsworth Primary School, Emsworth

Gentle But Chaotic Looloo

My monster's fur is...
A huge puffy, soft, fluffy ball.
Soft fuzzy bunny rabbits, hopping in the breeze.
A scrummy, yummy ball of candyfloss.

My monster's eyes are...
Glamourous, shimmering moons.
Glowing into the wavy Atlantic Ocean.
Gleaming stars in the dusk sky.
Shining pearls lying on the seabed.

My monster's tail is a...
Huge ball of cotton fun wagging.
Curled octopus tentacles on the seabed.
Octopus tentacles wiggling in the deep, dark sea.

My monster's belly is a...
Blue and pink bath bomb fizzing.
Huge teddy bear at the funfair.
Bowl of popcorn popping before the movies.

Emily Fuller (9)
Emsworth Primary School, Emsworth

A Fluffy Friend

My monster's eyes are glowing
Torches shining brightly,
His legs are a giraffe's neck
Stretching up for food up a tree.
His fuzzy, cuddly fur spreads
All over his body.
My monster's feet are enormous and huge
And the size of a bird flying.
His soft, gentle fur gently blows
In the cool breeze.
Finally, his claws are razor-sharp
Crocodile teeth chomping his prey.
My monster's ears are rounder
Than a coffee cup.
His teeth are a bull's sharp horns
His tongue is a bird's beak
Pecking at his seeds.
My monster's movement is a cheetah
Zooming through the wind.

Megan Edgington (8)
Emsworth Primary School, Emsworth

Fluffy Princess

His eyebrows are fuzzy felt, from a coat's hood.
His spots are stains from a leaky manor.
The monster's nose is a green pickle.
The Fluffy Princess's arms are purple pillows.
The monster's mouth is carpet.
The Fluffy Princess's eyes are blue pillows.
The monster's tummy is a bed that children can
bounce on.
The monster's hair is purple string.
His hands are feathers that you can stick on paper.
His body is a duster to get the dust off the rooms.
His doll is a spider doll, that has a pet spider.
His doll's house is a spider home.
His toy box is a mansion.

Roxy Thomson (8)
Emsworth Primary School, Emsworth

Bubble

My monster's eyes are...
Gleaming stars in the dark sky.
Glistening diamonds in the dark mine.
Shimmering pearls on the seabed.

My monster's fur is...
Soft, fuzzy bunny rabbits moving in the summer breeze.
Scrummy, yummy balls of cotton candy.
Woolly slippers next to a warm winter fire.

My monster's tail is a...
Huge ball of fluffy wagging.
Octopus tentacles wriggling in the deep sea.
A curled-up marshmallow.

My monster's belly is a...
Hot cross bun baking at Easter.
Huge teddy bear at the funfair.
Blue fizzy bath bomb.

Amelie Stratton (8)
Emsworth Primary School, Emsworth

Sinister Minister

His eyes are red fiery bombs
Exploding in the beautiful distance.
His hair is electric eels
In the dark gloomy water.
His nose is a mammoth-sized giraffe's neck
His eyebrows are dark mammoths
Stamping his head in black puddles.
His scars are a lion's scars
From fighting in a battle.
His neck is a tough group of elephants
Stampeding along.
His snake legs wriggle
As he walks, bobbing along.
His spiky hair jiggles with might
Like a tiger's fur when he's running.
His legs are jellyfish legs
As he strolls along.

Jack Chapman (8)
Emsworth Primary School, Emsworth

Atrocious Devil Shape-Shifter

This devil monstrosity, Abboo
Will not like you,
As he's a shape-shifter
Don't fall for his tricks.
He'll lure you with poisoned Weetabix.
His long nails will dig in your skin.
He will throw you in the bin
Like you're nothing but rubbish.
Only if you're unlucky.
He'll spit slime on you one hundred times.
He will make sure you go blind.
Don't forget, stay away!
Look out, his feet are like mice.
So small, yet so quiet,
He can really cause a riot.
Don't look away!
Watch out, he's about!

Imogen Brock (9)
Emsworth Primary School, Emsworth

Monster Myth

He will slither under your bed at night.
Kiss your parents goodnight.

His kiss, so strong you'll die of love.
Play with him, or you'll be swallowed whole.
His teeth are so sharp you won't survive.
He will take your parents' guts out
Use it as food.
You'll be with them monster rules.

He can hear you screaming inside
As his ears are so big.
He can't see you as his mask is too tight.
With three legs to catch you.

But be warned.
Still, don't worry. It's only a myth
Or is it?

Ellie-Mai Clift (10)
Emsworth Primary School, Emsworth

Fangster

Fangster's heart is bigger than a galaxy.
Fangster's hair is red, pointy devils.
Fangster's ears are spiky, long, fierce daggers.
Fangster's mouth is a dangerous white shark.
Fangster's tongue is a dusty basement in the
house of his mouth.
Fangster's arms sway in the powerful wind.
Fangster's legs wiggle whilst he walks with
thunderous steps.
Fangster's a shape-shifter, with hair like a
porcupine.
Fangster's fangs are daggers carrying blood.
Fangster's eyes are pools of glistening, terrifying
energy.

Rhodri Miller (8)

Emsworth Primary School, Emsworth

Frosty And His Pet Bean

Frosty is a hairy, scary monster.
His head is a huge ball.
His hair is spiky,
Spikier than the spikiest prickle bush.
His claws are sharp kitchen knives.
He has a horrible mouth
Which is a slimy, slobbery slug.
Indeed he has colossal eyes.
Sometimes they are pools of lava,
Sometimes they are big windows.
He has got a tail with prickles all over
Which is sharper than plates.
His pet, Bean, has a body as bony as a dog's
bony legs.
Bean has a cape as thin as the thinnest paper.
He is a miniature doll.

Jack Stephen Johnson (8)
Emsworth Primary School, Emsworth

Lazy Looloo

Her wide eyes are glistening
Beautiful amber sunsets.

Her eyes are shimmering rock pools,
Glimmering fireballs.

Long hairy clouds.
Listen to all the growls.

She is a large cheetah sprinting,
A hungry hyena howling,
A lazy leopard laughing.

She screams, shouts and giggles,
Now and then she wiggles.

Her circular belly
Is a little chunk of jelly.

Looloo's nose peeks.
Her rosy little cheeks
Are perfect petite petals.

Ailsa Fishwick (9)
Emsworth Primary School, Emsworth

My Monster

My monster's eyes are glamorous, shimmering
moons sparkling in the sky.
Silver stars glowing in the pitch-black.
Rainbow ribbons hanging down from a grand tree.

My monster is quick, just like a leopard sprinting
past the finish line.
Jumping like a kangaroo in the steaming hot
desert.

My monster is a graceful ballerina twirling in a
show.
Wearing funky strawberry lace bell earrings.
With slippery snakes sliding everywhere and
wobbly jelly just like at my birthday party.

Grace Margaret Davies (8)
Emsworth Primary School, Emsworth

Fluffo The Cuddly Monster

My monster's skin is a cuddly, soft puppy
Bouncing around the fields.

My monster's eyes are glamorous stars
Shimmering in the moonlight.

Fluffo's spots are scented bubblegum
Which makes you want to eat sweets.

Fluffo's tongue is a slippery slide
With water pouring out like a fountain.

His legs are like a cheetah
Chasing his prey.

His feet are adorable, cute like teddies
Wrapping around his friends all night long.

Lotti Chamberlain (9)
Emsworth Primary School, Emsworth

Sweetie Spider

My monster has melted, oozing earrings.
Her eyes are pools of gingerbread girls.
She has fingers that are marshmallows.
Her arms are blueberry and chocolate syrup.

She has spider legs that are turquoise blue,
And they are curled beautifully.
Her feet are sweet lemons
Sprinkled with chocolate.

Her body is a unicorn
Filled with strawberries.
Her eyelashes are thick bars.
Her tail is a squishy jelly snake,
Soaring high in the sky.

Lucy Ingleby
Emsworth Primary School, Emsworth

Butterfly Spot's Bow

My monster's skin is a ball of fluff.
It is a spotty Dalmatian,
Lying in a meadow in spring.

My monster's eyes are a playful puppy
Darting between its toys.

My monster's wings are a butterfly
Flapping in a cool breeze.

My monster's arms are fluffy balls
Rolling towards you.

My monster's legs are fluffy,
As fluffy as a bunny.

My monster's bow is a silky
Bunch of spiderwebs.

Leila Sprackling (8)
Emsworth Primary School, Emsworth

Rainbow The Monster

Rainbow the monster has an extended tail
When it hits the ground it shakes.
Her claws are sharp knives, but she doesn't
use them.
Her ears are the dark blue ocean.
Her eyes are two holes full of dirt.
Her belly is a bottomless pit.
Her teeth are two marshmallows.
Her skin is a dazzling rainbow.
Her legs are two miniature branches.
Her arms are two chocolate bars.
She has spiky swords poking out of her belly
to protect her.

Chloe Rosa Traill (8)

Emsworth Primary School, Emsworth

Scarforce

He smells his prey
From miles away.
Hides under your bed,
Your covers are red.
No time to run,
You're done.
He's fast like a cheetah
One of his legs is bone and the other skin.
His favourite food is every human.
Roar!
For he sees you.
His teeth are sharp
Like the tip of a sword,
Ready to bite!
His eyes are droopy
A deep scar goes through them
Like scissors cutting through paper.

Finley James Rowett (11)
Emsworth Primary School, Emsworth

The Seven-Horned Terror

The fire flames rise,
The seven horns are seen
And the fire eyes glow.

When you sleep, he finds you
Then feeds on your blood.
The human-eating, fire-breathing terror
Is near at all times.

When he sees your head,
The next thing you know you'll be dead.
When you're in bed and see red
You know you're in trouble
Because he's heard you
And now he's coming!

Mackenzie Thomson (10)
Emsworth Primary School, Emsworth

Mean Monster

My monster's eyes are
Melons coming to crash down onto Earth.
Fireballs burning red hot.
Fiery red balls, burning the world.

My monster's nails are
Mouldy, disgusting carrots.
Square crackers covered in brick.
Long pointy claws.

My monster's temper is
Like my brother when I attack him.
A ferocious lion growling.
A car engine growling powerfully.

Charlotte Sly (8)
Emsworth Primary School, Emsworth

It's Coming!

It is skulking through the night
Seeking out its prey.
Going to give you a major fright!

It is coming and creeping,
Now it's getting closer,
You are petrified and weeping!

Here comes your fate,
It's closing around you,
You're not supposed to be bait!

It is skulking through the night
Seeking out its prey.
Going to give you a major fright!

Quiola Arthur (9)
Emsworth Primary School, Emsworth

Scary Monster

Smelly, crazy, ugly Bob.
Cheeky, naughty monster.
He will get in your bed
When you are fast asleep.
Snoring his head off in a deep sleep.
He can become invisible,
Go through walls
When you are sleeping.
He may seem nice
But you'd be surprised.
He will dance on your bed
But might chop off your head.
Shh! Be quiet! Stop!
Look behind you! There's Bob!

Haydon Skeates (10)
Emsworth Primary School, Emsworth

All About Rocker Pumpkin

His head is an orange fiery pumpkin.
His guitar is a blue rocking lightning rhino.
His shirt is a pitch-black spotty shirt.
His leaves fall off every second,
With the guitar knocking it off.
His amp is a rumbling lion.
His teeth are bloody vampire fangs.
His eyes are crossed on his pumpkin head.
His nose is a spiky, rhino horn.
His pumpkin head is a rotten tomato head.

Kyle Holly (8)
Emsworth Primary School, Emsworth

Haunted Boy

His feet are amazing footballs.
His eyes are balls of flames.
His tummy is full of meat.
His hands are shark teeth.
His ears are knives.
His teeth are daggers.
His knees are invisible.
His elbows are rock.
He has lightning speed.
His hair is fire.
He is as strong as a gorilla.
He is a fireball of flames
His back is a bunch of volcanoes.

Freddie Gosling (8)
Emsworth Primary School, Emsworth

Bobalop The Monster

Her face makes you want to eat it
And she smells of cupcakes.
Her eyes are huge beach balls,
Spinning round and round.
Her sprinkles are rainbow-coloured
Dots on her red face.
Her arms are wiggly jelly in the air.
The monster's ears are blue sharp teeth.
Bobalop's feet are cats' claws,
Sharp and pointy.
Her body is a square cake.

Sofia Cox (8)
Emsworth Primary School, Emsworth

The Wisey Wise

Her eyes flow with water
While her fingers crinkle up
In the sparkling water.
Her belly is rumbling thunder.
Her face is a pizza,
With freckles she can breathe through.
Her face turns into a turquoise puddle.
Her legs are saws that won't stop slicing.
Her words are always written on her cheeks.
Her legs are always runny just like a centipede.

Grace Cooper (8)
Emsworth Primary School, Emsworth

Fluffy'o Monster

His pumpkin body,
More orange than a pumpkin,
Slowly rotting.

His green slimy tail
Thumping on the floor.
A monstrous beast!

His belly is a bottomless pit
Of deconstructed buildings.
His skin is flaming orange.

He's a cute baby puppy.
His wings the size of hawks.
His head is a globe
That acts as a body.

Zack Goodman (8)
Emsworth Primary School, Emsworth

Dinotaur

Dinotaur is in my garden
I don't know what to do.
Dinotaur is in my garden
I don't want to move.
I'm going to try to scare him,
I know what he's going to do.
He's not moving, but I need to move.
I run to the den,
And when I look again
He is not there.
Where is my Dinotaur?
Where? Out there?

Joe Gallagher (9)
Emsworth Primary School, Emsworth

Mr Big Mouth

My monster's tongue is...
A slimy snail, slithering on a leaf.
A bumpy pencil writing.

My monster's legs are...
Blankets that haven't been used yet.
A rock that's been smashed into bits.

My monster's eyes are...
A huge monster eye poured on with bleach
A slug moving around your skin.

Aiden David Shale (8)
Emsworth Primary School, Emsworth

Fluffy Chequed

His two puny legs are aqua-dashed indigo cushions.
His two blush eyes are shimmering, sunny, pink paint buckets.
His majestic marmalade cheeks are coral pumpkin skin.
His unsighted, titchy mouth is a scandalous ebony iPad case.
His circular, round body shape is the middle of a doughnut.
His dim, specked pupils are crushed Oreos.

Lenny Robinson (8)
Emsworth Primary School, Emsworth

Rainbow The Fluffy Monster

I can smell body spray from Rainbow
Who sprayed it in my bedroom
It smells like cotton candy

I can see Rainbow lying underneath my bed
Waiting for me to get out of bed
So we can play together

I can taste bubblegum in my thoughts
The bubbles pop and tickle as Rainbow moves
Rainbow is my best friend.

Amelia Twigger (10)
Emsworth Primary School, Emsworth

My Monster

My monster's eyes are stars
Blinking in the dark blue sky.
They are emeralds shimmering
In a precious jewellery box.
His fur is a lovely new teddy bear
Snuggled up in bed.
He is a bald, fierce lion
Roaring in a field.
My monster's teeth are sharp like knives
Cutting fish in tiny pieces.

Arabelle Chloe Clark (8)
Emsworth Primary School, Emsworth

Snuggles The Monster!

Snuggles!
My monster is cute.
My monster is adorable.
My monster is big and fluffy.
My monster is really bouncy.
My monster is called Snuggles.
My monster is very snuggly.
My monster is also very cuddly.
My monster is amazing.
My monster buzzes like a bee
When she cuddles up with me.

Iga Boczon (9)
Emsworth Primary School, Emsworth

Pumpkin The Halloween Monster

The sun shines down on her
Beautiful, shiny, fluffy fur.

Her eyelashes are long spiders,
Crawling on the only eye she has.

Her antenna can look very far,
Very far away for a mirror
To look at her stunning face.

Her eyes are gorgeous
Shining blue gems
On her stunning face.

Isabelle Kendall (9)
Emsworth Primary School, Emsworth

Sprinkle The Slimy Monster

I am Sprinkle.
I am very fluffy and I am covered in rainbows.
I have been told that I smell
Of candyfloss and fresh doughnuts.
As a monster, I love to eat.
But don't worry - not humans!
Doughnuts and cake!
I leave a trail of rainbows.
I am as fluffy as a unicorn's mane.

Evie Stratford Burden (10)

Emsworth Primary School, Emsworth

Squiggle Squarebottom

Short and naughty with curly horns,
Stares at you with one big eye.
Squiggle Squarebottom is a cheeky monkey.
Scoots down the road with a scooter
Especially made for him.
Steals people's wallets
And belongings as he passes by.
No time to sleep even if you try
Otherwise, you might die.

Seth Piper (11)
Emsworth Primary School, Emsworth

My Monster

My monster's eyes are slippery slimy bogeys.
My monster's teeth are sharp knives cutting vegetables.
My monster's hair is a grizzly bear.
He is a slimy slug, slithering across the street.
His legs are hairy black spiders, crawling around the room.

Aiden Austin (8)

Emsworth Primary School, Emsworth

Beware!

When you hear your hallways creak,
He's coming for you.
When you hear the walls scratching,
He's sharpening his claws.
When you hear the dripping,
There is blood!
When you hear him purr,
He is underneath your bed!

Harvey Dowling (9)
Emsworth Primary School, Emsworth

Pink Poppy

Pink Poppy is scary in the daytime.
She can fly through the playground.
She hides behind the bins and trees.
Her eyes can glow
Make sure you don't make a sound,
Pink Poppy monster is looking around.

Emily Silk (9)
Emsworth Primary School, Emsworth

Dark Fright

He chomps and munches.
He leaves your fridge
Flat in his tracks
As he extracts
Food from life.
Never look back
Terror will be in your track.
His mouth is like a forest of teeth.

Charlie Carver (10)
Emsworth Primary School, Emsworth

In The Night

At night, Spike gives you a fright,
While sneaking into your bedroom,
While eating your teddies.
While leaving spikes behind.
Leaving nightmares behind.
Strange things in your bedroom.

Brandon-Lee Stuart Gray (9)
Emsworth Primary School, Emsworth

In The Midnight Darkness

In the midnight darkness,
One hundred stars in the navy blue sky,
Something shadowed in-between
The twisty, curvy tree.
It opened one eye.
A beast that stole lives.

In the midnight darkness,
This beast will murder
People, animals and anything else.
Piercing through the misty woods,
No one knows his name.
Someone is walking past,
Whoever it may be,
"Yeti," someone shouts
And then runs like a herd
Of wild horses racing a train.

In the midnight darkness,
Cosy in his bed.
His stumpy legs,
Fat body, round head.

Now jump in and close your eyes,
Make sure you visualise,
The yeti in his comfy bed.

Daisy Johnson (8)
Kirtlington CE Primary School, Kirtlington

The Super Smash

No one can see it because it's dark.
It can go around the world in less than one second.
Fists as big as the body.
It is dark, even when light is shining you can't see it.
It hunts even though the wind blows hard.
When the sun goes down, everyone tucks up.
Hide underneath their beds so they don't get eaten.
When the night goes past, the sun comes up.
Everyone is relieved they're not in a tummy and can't see.
It's sharp and nobody wants to be near it.
It can see the trees because it's taller than the clouds.
It can go up and down.
Its bones are cracked in his legs
It can take them out and throw them
And they come back.

Char Darke (8)
Kirtlington CE Primary School, Kirtlington

The No Face

At the bottom of my garden, in the shed,
There was a monster that we thought dead.
Until one night it came out,
It wandered out towards our house,
Where we were all safe in bed.
It smashed down the door.
From my bed, I fell to the floor.
I awoke from my sleep,
In one small stroke of its massive hand,
It struck down a wall,
The house crashed down.
The feet of the monster crushed the bits of
the wall.
It rampaged down the street
Causing chaos with its giant feet.
Through the madness,
Through the destruction,
Its evil plan was in action.

Will Langrish (9)
Kirtlington CE Primary School, Kirtlington

The Beast Of Black And Yellow

The mythical vines lay gently above my head,
Dreaming of sleeping in my blankety bed.
Nests of death hanging over my neck
Fearing the beast will awake the doom of my
death.

Spiking pins shoot into my veins
Piercing the life of the hammering rain.
Trickling gore ran down my face,
Moving slowly at a calm but violent pace.

Stretches of yellow ran across its back,
The rest of black ran between its inner gaps.
Wings of white flap instantly
Standing out in the night of black.

Isabelle Houselander (9)
Kirtlington CE Primary School, Kirtlington

Death...

Wild Fierce Hairy, are the yeti's middle names.
Call him Mr Moody.
It's sure to go down in vain.
Screech!
Howled a violin rushing through my ears.
For he has woken again.
Yes he has woken again.
He who is the Yeti.
A red pool he stands in.
Dripping from the mouth
It dripped, dripped, into Hell.

I never advise you to go.
For he will eat you whole.
Never go near.
Now never go near
As this is the end of your life...

Holly Cole (9)
Kirtlington CE Primary School, Kirtlington

The Almighty Fly By Night

Deep in flight
Was the Fly By Night.
He had a glorious mane
And he was never in pain.
For this is the almighty Fly By Night.

Living in the hills,
Hiding away until
The night was dark
And the land was stark.

When people were in trouble
He would be there on the double.
From his giant paws and heroic face
Everyone knew he would never lose a race.
Now, you shouldn't worry when he is here,
For he will wipe away all of your fear!

Lola Jenkins (10)
Kirtlington CE Primary School, Kirtlington

The Unnamed

Howling wind shook the night,
Wolves and foxes growled.
But something else defeated their might...
It scowled.

Emerging from plaited houses
Its stomping paws trudged closer.
It took a moment for my eyes to see,
A beast twisting, turning like a roller coaster.

Prickled fur stuck up out of a car-sized body,
Climbing up to oval ears.
An open mouth gripped onto holly
I ran, the crunching was terrible to hear!

Aria Miller (9)
Kirtlington CE Primary School, Kirtlington

V Shape Dust Guy

He always eats the Vs out the alphabet tin.
He has a friend called Halloween Gummy Bear.
His smile is not an ordinary smile, it is a V smile!
Whenever you tickle him, he will be very ticklish.
He only has three pieces of hair on his head
Because he cut the rest off.
His famous feet would stomp-alompa
He loves the letter V
It's his favourite letter of the alphabet.
That's why his name is V Shape Dust Guy.

Ayla Mansell (9)
Kirtlington CE Primary School, Kirtlington

The Legendary Serpent

In the dark blanket of the night,
Children tucked up tight
Safely in their bed.
For in the thrashing waves
There emerged a head.
Scales moved swiftly in the water.
Getting ready to slaughter.
Fins sliced through the foam,
Followed by a painful groan.
Twisting, knotting and churning,
Houses kept on burning
Until it was ash and rubble.
It moved on, there was no more trouble.

Seth Flood (9)
Kirtlington CE Primary School, Kirtlington

Slither Never Gets Defeated

The waves splashed against the sandy shore
Over the rumble, we heard a roar.

The beast crawled forward
Slimy and vile, waiting to pounce.

Thin, mean eyes,
A heart of stone,
Teeth sharp and deadly.

From my feet to my head,
I turn hard and grey, frozen,
Paralysed in stone.

One hour later,
I'm a pile of ash,
Never to be heard of again.

Lucy Charlesworth (9)
Kirtlington CE Primary School, Kirtlington

Death Of Spike

The wind howled in the face of citizens
As the monster roamed the city.
His slimy, oozing eyes making people blind.
A figure appeared from the moonlight,
It was a fright.
When suddenly it turned white.
I just got very tight.
His tail squeezing me till the day
That I will be afraid
To take him on.
So I'm afraid
For the day
That I'm going to die.

Zach Bradney (9)
Kirtlington CE Primary School, Kirtlington

Crimeria

At the core of Earth, Crimeria stirred from his heated sleep.
He pushed his way through, rock, earth and sand.
Crimeria bobbed up to the top of the sea, sweating as he went.
Hot as magma lava to the unknown beast of the underworld.
His brain is the size of a pea, but he knew to kill with poo.
His trusted fingers crept up to the tower bridge.
He ate human soup.

Alex Grebot (9)
Kirtlington CE Primary School, Kirtlington

The Killersaurus

The slithering beast would slither all day, all night.
One bite, that's you gone. You might even turn
white.
When it happens, you'll spout blood.
The more you scream, the stronger it gets.
It feeds on screams and children's flesh.
It steams when hot and freezes when cold.
His eyes, ruby-red, as hot as the sun.

Sam Bartlett (8)
Kirtlington CE Primary School, Kirtlington

Liontor

In the dark, dark night
The beast stared in the jet-black hole deep in the
ground.
The sound of roaring while the wolves tried to
scare it away.
The sound of howling as the sharp, triangular
things
In its mouth dug into its prey.
The thump of its feet, the shake of the ground.
The Liontor has hit town.

Ernie Emmerson (8)
Kirtlington CE Primary School, Kirtlington

Halloween

The beast attempted to slaughter its prey.
Under the cold white blanket of snow
It devoured its frozen meat silently.
The cold, misty night
Children asleep in their cosy beds
But the Halloween nightmares
Are out tonight.
Turns out I got the ultimate nightmare.
The yeti was real.

Dotty Dartnell (8)
Kirtlington CE Primary School, Kirtlington

The Headless Yeti

One stormy night,
Under the chestnut tree,
Lived a legendary beast
That woke to feast.
That beast was headless,
Red eyes burning hot,
Roar that shatters glass,
He can put his head on his hand.
He punches snow with his feet,
This beast you wouldn't want to meet.

James Allison (8)
Kirtlington CE Primary School, Kirtlington

Night Terror

The Night was as dark as the sea.
Bigger than one hundred skyscrapers.
Faster than light.
It travels the world spying on its prey.
One terrifying night it comes from the ground,
A horn harder than bedrock
And a huge appetite for meat.
Stealthier than a ninja.

Finley Mundy (9)
Kirtlington CE Primary School, Kirtlington

The Monster

A hill emerged,
A mound of earth,
Monster turf.
Bursting out
Without a doubt
A terrifying sight.
Run away,
Scream they did.
None could help.
From his mouth
Came a yelp.
His breath blew out
He screeched his words
Heard by all.

Arthur Dartnall (10)
Kirtlington CE Primary School, Kirtlington

The Monster Beware

Inside your house, look under your bed
And you might see a 'teddy'.
If you pick it up you will be surprised...
But don't worry because it is friendly.
It's purple, fluffy and soft.
She likes to sleep and make friends.
She also likes to play.
In hide-and-seek, beware, she's a shape-shifter
And hides in your teddies.
She likes to turn into cute animals
And write about it.

She looks like a teddy bear
Who is as small as a baby
And as friendly as a newborn puppy.
But most of all, she's as fast
As a cheetah so good luck in tag!

When she speaks it sounds like a cat
And when she walks you don't even realise,
You might be scared a couple of times.

Saxony-Brook Betts (10)
Marsh Lane Primary School, Marsh Lane

My Mate Gruff

This morning I find a rip in my bed,
A slash in my curtains and a scratch on my head...
I get ready to read because it's almost night,
Oh dear, oh dear, I'm in for a fright.

I hear the door open, he climbs up the stairs,
Then walks into my room like he doesn't care.
What am I doing? I need to run,
But he looks so friendly, almost like my mum.

I jump out of bed not daring to blink.
He smiles at me, then gives me a wink.
"Oh gosh, oh help me find a friend,
I feel that my life's going to soon end."

I introduce him to my parents and we become mates.
I'm not that scared after all but hope not to be ate.
So some beasts are friendly, especially Gruff.
So don't judge a monster by its looks, it might not be rough!

But just be careful of what you do
'Cause some of them aren't like that, they even go boo!
So remember this child, lock the door!
'Cause it will be waiting for your little snore.

Mya Grace Jans (10)

Marsh Lane Primary School, Marsh Lane

Spike The Closet Monster

This is my night diary,
I know that it's quite frightening,
But this is what it's like for me,
To get out of bed to do a wee.

Spike is the closet monster,
He lives in my wardrobe,
He puts on anything he finds
Even the stuff that goes under the clothes.

Every night he opens the door
Looking for smelly socks on the floor.
Every time he finds a sock,
All you can hear is 'scoff, scoff, scoff'.

Spike the closet monster,
Hangs my pants on his horns,
But there is one thing I don't know,
Does he wear the ones that I've worn?

So the lesson I'm trying to teach you,
Is don't drop your stinky socks on the floor,

Or you will see a spiky monster,
Open up your closet door...

Joseph Hobson (10)

Marsh Lane Primary School, Marsh Lane

I'm Jerry

I'm a friendly monster,
I'm as small as monsters go.
I'm blue with red cow spots,
But there's something you should know.

My eyes are round and big,
Though no friends I can see,
If you can help me get a friend,
Oh, how grateful I would be.

I've finally found a friend,
Life doesn't seem so bad,
Despite the trial and error,
I love my new friend, Chad.

You have brought me joy
And lots of happiness,
But the most important thing is
You've taken away my loneliness.

Natalie Graham (10)
Marsh Lane Primary School, Marsh Lane

The Monster

With slashes in my curtains,
Scratches on my wall,
There lay a monster,
Snoring in bed.
I look in my cupboard,
Nothing is there,
I hear a sound
From somewhere.
I open the window,
The monster woke up,
The noise was coming from outside,
A man was running,
Running away.
The monster grabbed me by the arm.
I thought I was going to get eaten,
But he gave me a big hug.
He said, "I'm here now, I'm your friend."

Ruby May (11)
Marsh Lane Primary School, Marsh Lane

Morphias The Laughing Monster

Make sure to lock your doors and windows at night
Make sure to lock them oh so tight.
Because if you don't, you're just waiting for a fright
And be the monster's breakfast to his delight.
He chuckles.
He laughs
All night long.
His mouth is an infinite abyss
And watch out for his sticky tongue.
He waits under your bed
Waiting for you to wake.
He waits.
He waits.
And when you get up
You will finally meet your fate.

Joshua Hebb (10)
Marsh Lane Primary School, Marsh Lane

Cheesos

Cheesos is loyal.
Cheesos is friendly.
Cheesos is stinky.
When he tries to make friends
They run off on the road with big bends.
One day a boy saw him stinking away,
Scaring all the kids away.
He was lonely, he had no one to play with.
One day, the boy made a change.
He gave him a bath.
Now he does not stink of cheese
And has no fleas or knobbly knees.
He is just a friendly block of cheese.

Bailey Harrison Williams (10)
Marsh Lane Primary School, Marsh Lane

Bob

Bob is very mean
Because he has sharp fangs
To eat people.

He is very scary
Because when all the street lights are all off
He walks out in the middle of the night.

Bob has orange and black pointy horns
On top of his head.
He has a big fat belly.

Bob is as fast as a cheetah
And as scary as a rhino opening his mouth.
When Bob walks on the floor
It sounds like a dinosaur.

Dylan Millington (10)
Marsh Lane Primary School, Marsh Lane

Goofy Goff

Goofy Woofy was a silly banana,
He eats his food up, like a piranha.

He goes downstairs to watch some TV.
Goofy goes to get some popcorn.
He eats it all up.
Now he has no corn.

Yummy,
Mummy,
For my tummy.
Get off my bed.

Goofy Goff has a red cape
With a yellow badge in the middle,
He gets wrapped in tape
Stuck to a lamp post.

Lily-Mae Coulson (10)
Marsh Lane Primary School, Marsh Lane

The Monster Is Lurking

One night
I had a rip in my bed,
A rip in my clothes
And a cut in my head.

I opened my door.
I thought there was a monster out there,
The pants were everywhere.

Big Sid was scared of the human upstairs.
Sid looked up and the human looked down.
Sid walked up and the human walked down.
Sid was not scared anymore.

Zach Burdett (10)
Marsh Lane Primary School, Marsh Lane

Night House

In an abandoned house lies the thing of your
nightmares.
If you enter you don't leave.
His growl is like thunder.
His teeth draw blood like needles.
He emerges from rooms like a shadow.
Many have tried to kill him
But he is the untamed predator.
Bone after bone, skull and all.
As he escapes
A sacred ritual will ban his soul.

Thomas George Evison (10)
Marsh Lane Primary School, Marsh Lane

Big Fluffy Monster

The monster called Big Fluffy Monster,
When he sees kids
He will chase them until they die.
Big Fluffy Monster will devour them for supper.
Then he will go out for more.
He will chase them for ages, again and again.
Day and night.
Twenty-four-seven.
Then there will be no more people left.

Alfie Marshall (10)
Marsh Lane Primary School, Marsh Lane

The Night-Time Horror

Every night from under your bed,
The Moon Lord needs to be fed.
The kids squawk and squirm
While the Moon Lord is quite firm.
It feeds off kids who are scared,
Sadly, it can't be scared.

Micah Burlaga (10)
Marsh Lane Primary School, Marsh Lane

The Shadowy Beast

It was Halloween night,
I had just finished trick or treating with my friends,
I looked at my clock, the hands pointing directly at
twelve.
Surely it couldn't be that late?
I closed my eyes for a bit and, like a flash,
I was off to the land of nod.

But not for long,
Something woke me up, I don't know how, I don't
know what,
As soon as my eyes adjusted to the pitch-black
room,
I turned around and looked at my alarm clock.
Oh no! 3am! The witching hour!
As soon as I thought it couldn't get any worse,
I heard an eerie growl,
Maybe it was Dad snoring? But no!
I heard an unusual creak from the floorboard,
Down the dimly-lit hallway.
Suddenly a shadow emerged from the darkness.

There were millions of questions in my head,
Should I run? Should I hide?
I quickly but quietly got my hockey stick,
Now I had a weapon.

Shaking, I looked down the hallway,
And realised it was not, therefore, a monster.
But just my dog Tom, his stomach rumbling,
Looking for something to eat!

Holly Horner (10)
Saints & Scholars Integrated Primary School, Armagh

Monsters' Fright

I was standing in my bedroom when I got quite a
fright,
I got really scared as it was Halloween night,
Oh why tonight, why not Easter?
I took my nightgown and put on my slipper.
I went downstairs and opened the door,
I could not believe what was on the kitchen floor!
Standing there were four shiny eyes,
Staring back at me in surprise.
Two creatures, one green, one yellow,
With both mouths full of Jell-O.
One was small, one was tall
And there was food splattered on the wall.
They told me they were hungry and said, "Thanks
for the food.
We needed energy, sorry for being rude.
Our names are Blobb and Bot-Bot, and we are
from Planet Bong.
Now you have helped us, we'll sing our goodbye
song.
Bleep. Blop. Bloop. Blup. Bong-ey. Boon.
We must go, see you soon!"

They went up in their silver spaceship,
I waved goodbye and wished them a nice trip.

Sophie Bradley (9)
Saints & Scholars Integrated Primary School, Armagh

What's In My Wardrobe

What's in my wardrobe?
Who's there with my bathrobe?
What is that roaring?
Is it just my dad snoring?
As quick as a flash I opened the door,
To find a massive *Roooaaaar!*
I looked down to see,
What could it be?
Then I saw a chubby, tiny thing,
And that thing started to sing!
It was very furry,
Not one bit scary.
It had a question mark on its belly,
And it was eating jelly.
It whimpered like a dog
And jumped like a frog.
It screamed, "Arghhhhhh!"
And I screamed, "Arghhhhhh!"
It had two wobbly antennae,
And one sparkling green eye.

So I asked, "What's your name?"
And it replied, "How did you know?"

Odette O'Donnell (9)

Saints & Scholars Integrated Primary School, Armagh

Socky The Little Monster

There once was a little monster,
Who lived under Max's bed.
The monster's name was Socky
And he liked smelly socks.
At night when Max was sleeping
He crept out of the dark
And sniffed around the room
To find his favourite stuff.
All kinds of different socks
Which Max loved to throw around.
Socks blue, red and orange,
Socks glowing green in the dark.
But favourite of them all,
Were the ones which smelt a lot.
He put them in a pile
And made a stinky bed.
Then lay down for a nap
But slept till the end of night.

Hera Araja (9)
Saints & Scholars Integrated Primary School, Armagh

Bobby

With a head like a blueberry,
Arms like sticks,
Crawls through the park.
Slipping and whooping,
He zooms down the slide.

His belly starts to rumble,
As he hunts through the bins.
Bang goes the lids,
As he dives in to find
Any old cabbage leaves left behind.

Stuffing his face like a dirty old pig,
Ketchup dripping down his mouth,
Licking his lips and squealing with delight,
The scary wee alien disappears in the night.

Kate Grimley (9)
Saints & Scholars Integrated Primary School, Armagh

Slimy Sid

Once there lived Slimy Sid, lonely in his lair,
Until one day he went out for fingers and fresh air.
He wandered down the street at night,
He followed one bright light,
To find some children tucked up tight
And ate all their fingers
For his next few dinners.
But maybe someday Sid will learn,
The only fingers he truly likes
Are locked up in the freezer,
Guarded by hungry mice.

Beth Erin Patrick (9)
Saints & Scholars Integrated Primary School, Armagh

Who's There?

What's that over there?
The rustling of the blind cords.
Sounds like they're trying to warn.
The creaking of the floorboard.

Flinching of my body,
Sweat dripping off my head,
Hand soaking.

Left and right,
Thoughts racing through my head.
Who is it?
What is it?
Who's there?

Aalia Donnelly (11)
Saints & Scholars Integrated Primary School, Armagh

My Monster

My Monster is called Frankenstein.
He is One of the kindest monsters in the world.
He Never goes to sleep.
He is as Spotty as a giraffe.
He is so big - bigger Than a giant.
He is the silliest monster Ever.
His tummy is the Roundest you've ever seen.

Mia Ewart (10)

Saints & Scholars Integrated Primary School, Armagh

My Despicable Spike

My monster is called Spike,
He rides a bike
And he strikes in the night.
So watch out for night.
Spike is very giant
And roars like a lion.
He is rotten
And likes to wear cotton.
His actions are despicable
And he makes his friends feel miserable.

Oliver (9)
Saints & Scholars Integrated Primary School, Armagh

The Little Monster

There was once a little monster
Who was not spooky and not nice
But was so pretty
And always as busy as a bee.
He was certainly not big,
He was very small
With little polka dots.
He would scare you, but not me,
He is so fluffy.
I love Fangs.

Aimee Murray (9)
Saints & Scholars Integrated Primary School, Armagh

In The Darkness Of The Night

In the darkness of the night,
The monsters lurk and wait to bite.
In the darkness of the night,
The monsters say,
"Come out little one, we want to play."
In the darkness of the night,
The monsters stay for all the fright.

Nathaniel Faulkner (10)
Saints & Scholars Integrated Primary School, Armagh

The Witch

I saw a black, scary cat,
It belonged to a witch who was very fat.
I saw the witch as she sat on my mat,
Then I saw her put on her pointy hat.
The witch left me a bright yellow pumpkin,
The fireworks exploded and we ran from
something.

Aine McCann-Wilson (9)
Saints & Scholars Integrated Primary School, Armagh

Mad Hungry Monster

Hungry Monster is very merry
When he goes on a ferry
With a derry.

Hungry Monster is super greedy.
He eats everything
Because he is needy.

Hungry Monster has poisonous arrows that are green.
When he gets angry, he becomes super mean.
On his chest, he has a magical crystal that is pink.
It helps protect him and makes him think.

Christopher Shaw (7)
St Helens PACE PRU, Parr

Monster Robot

Chemical Plant is a silver monster-robot.
He is hot and has two spots.
Chemical Plant likes to draw pictures and has
silver spikes.
They are like wheels of a trike.
My robot doesn't die if he touches ice.
He likes to roll his blue ice.
He's got a big mouth and it's blue.
He's got green teeth that look brand new.

Adrian Tomcik (7)
St Helens PACE PRU, Parr

My Monster

Spooky is an underwater ghost.
Spooky likes scaring reef sharks most.
Spooky sometimes likes to play in the mud.
Spooky always likes drinking red blood.
Spooky has a friend who is glad to be a bat.
Gloomy is his name, and he is often sad.

Charlie Unsworth (8)
St Helens PACE PRU, Parr

Noel The Sea Monster

Noel is a lad,
He feels very sad.

Noel is red,
He loves his bed.

Noel eats pasta
Like my dog, Rasta.

When Noel is in bed
He likes to cuddle Ted.

Leon Jones (6)
St Helens PACE PRU, Parr

Whale

Red has a friend called Ted,
Ted likes to go to bed.
Ted likes to sail on a whale.
Spotty the whale is very polite.
Spotty reads the mail in jail.
He has a spiky tail.

Joseph Anglesey-Mahoney (7)
St Helens PACE PRU, Parr

The Football Monster

Remi is a monster, and a friendly one too,
He wants to play football, just like you.
Every day he saw everyone
Playing football and having fun!
So one day, he gathered up his courage and kicked the ball,
But it missed the goal and flew over the wall!
The children let out the loudest scream,
One that would've made your ears turn green.
Remi started to say, "Oh, don't yell so. I only want to play.
Please, I'll do anything, if only you'll let me stay."

But his only reply was, "A creature like you?
You're scary and ugly and you dribble oozing goo!
You're probably the most intimidating creature of them all,
Not forgetting you lost our ball!"

Remi sat down and began to cry tears of goo,
I mean, how would you feel if things like that were said about you?
They trickled down his furry face and landed on his hand,

This gave him a sudden thought - yes!
A wonderful plan!
If you had been there, you would've felt excitement
bubbling up from beneath you,
Remi's tears landed in his cupped hands which
began to ooze with green goo.
In a few minutes, he had fashioned a new sphere.
"Come on guys!" he shouted. "I have a new ball
right here!"
He kicked his ball and it began to roll...
But this time it landed neatly in the goal!
"You scored! You scored!" the players cheered.
Maybe he wasn't the scary monster they had
feared.
The children hesitated before joining in,
But it was obvious that Remi's team was going to
win.

When the match was over, they lifted him into the
air,
"We love you monster," they shouted, "everyone,
everywhere!"

Anna Wilson (9)
St John Of Jerusalem CE Primary School, Hackney

The Jackal!

When night-time calls and people are asleep,
Monsters are lurking around and in every crew
There is always a jackal, and his name is Joker.
He runs crazily overnight and places his heart-
crushing claws inside many young children.
He twists his head back and forward,
Side to side, making horrible vomiting sounds
And interrupting children's dreams.

When daytime calls and people are awake,
He crawls back into this house and says
Some unusual phase, in his same evil voice,
"I will hunt you, and find you,
Even when you're in the loo.
I will make sure your friends die too.
I won't stop till the last cow moos,
You are mine and that is true!"

Nathan Minganu (9)
St John Of Jerusalem CE Primary School, Hackney

This Is My Monster

This is my monster,
Well, he's not really a monster,
But, well, he kind of is.
He's very skinny, his legs are short
And he has a nice big yellow grin.
In the morning his breath smells like rotten eggs
And in the evening, it smells like peaches.

This is my monster,
Well, he's not really a monster,
But, well, he kind of is.
His nose is red, his hands are too.
He's got long, thin, dangly arms.
Spiders weave in and out of his hair
And his eyes are a strange deep green.

This is my monster,
Well, he's not really a monster,
My monster is me.

Edward Skrine (10)
St John Of Jerusalem CE Primary School, Hackney

Monster Invasion

Joe and Bo were monsters,
They were crazy and amazing.
When I was three years old
I created the monsters.
I shouted, "Help!"
For my mum and dad.
He called the police and I said,
"The monsters were Play-Doh,
And now they're alive."
When he was five years old
He went to Year 1 with his mum.
He saw the big monster
Roaring at his mum.
The monster ate his mum
And then she was gone.
He was crying.
I felt sorry for my dad
Then I made Play-Doh.

Matthew Erhunnwunsee (9)
St John Of Jerusalem CE Primary School, Hackney

Bone Crusher

I snore and sleep in perfect peace,
Of happy things, I always dream.
I think of the blood of humans on my jaw.
Of their screams and shaking when I roar.
But wait!
I think there's an intruder
Inside my cave.
There's nothing ruder.
So, I guess it's time to crush some bones,
I'll laugh and dance and watch them moan
Because from my sleep they've woken me up.
So in my teeth, they will all be stuck.

Nathan Precilla (9)

St John Of Jerusalem CE Primary School, Hackney

Fluffy Breakfast Food

Oh Fluffy, oh Fluffy Bread, you'll have good meals.
Instead, he ran out of my kitchen
And had no time to say goodbye!
Dough was as sweet as sweet could be.
His creamy, fresh, yellow, sweet butter
Was not even scooped on yet.
"Argh!" said White Spotless Blank Plate,
"I don't want to be used!"
"Ha! You're not getting away now!"
But suddenly, he fell to the floor.

Paige Violet Blaxill (10)

St John Of Jerusalem CE Primary School, Hackney

The Shadow Monster

Every day and I mean every day,
I have to face the monster,
The Shadow Monster.
Bash! Bash! Crash! Crash!
Suddenly, I find out that when I throw my pillows
on him,
Slowly, he turns into...
A cute monster!
He calls himself Shadow,
From a planet called Zarrt
What a strange, odd creature!
But he just needed a pal,
And that pal was... me!

Chukwudi Favour Emmanuel-Echerenwa (9)

St John Of Jerusalem CE Primary School, Hackney

My Monster

My monster is from the Macroverse.
He is the eater of worlds,
He's in Earth right now.
Human flesh tastes better with fear,
And more easy to scare.
So that's why he mostly eats children.
His true form is unknown,
But humans see it as a giant spider.

Harley Holdip Henry (9)
St John Of Jerusalem CE Primary School, Hackney

Shortsie

Being a monster is so much fun.
Sometimes going out for a little run.
But when he comes home
He gets very excited for his
Large, fantastic hot-cross bun.
He has the longest tongue in the world.
Once he hurled over the world.
But most importantly,
He is as gentle as a feather.
And his name is Shortsie.

Patrick Phillips (10)
St Patrick's Primary School, Kilsyth

Ziggy The Monster

Z iggy is blue and pink, with sharp claws. He
I s the most dangerous monster that ever was.
He is
G ooey and spotty,
G reen sparkles and
Y ellow teeth.

T errifying.
H e has horns. He is the most
E xcellent

M onster
O n the Monster Earth.
N o monster is as
S uper as
T he monster, Ziggy. He lives on Monster
E arth with all the other monsters. He
R eads books most of the time.

Ellie Morrison (10)
St Patrick's Primary School, Kilsyth

Slimy Socks

S limy Socks is as stinky as a bin.

L ongest tongue in the world.

I will tell you, he is scary.

M y goodness! His teeth are as yellow as bananas.

Y ou can see a trail of slime.

S potty, slimy, shape-shifter.

O h my! He is as slimy as a slug.

C hildren hiding under their beds.

K ids running away.

S limy Socks is the best, but scariest monster in the world.

Zara Valentine Higney (9)
St Patrick's Primary School, Kilsyth

Hungry Harry

H mm, I am hungry, *mmm*, burgers.
U nder the cave, *stomp, stomp!*
N ever get enough, it's so good
G etting burgers every day.
R oaring like a dinosaur, I want more!
Y ou could hear me from the other side.

H ungry as Harry.
A s happy as Larry.
R oar! I want food!
R oar! I am still hungry!
Y ou have to give me food.

Aiden Gall (10)
St Patrick's Primary School, Kilsyth

Hungry Harry

Hungry Harry was crazy as could be,
He was rather particular, maybe, to see.
He had a dog's head, but a horse's body.
He was very naughty.
When he was hungry
You could hear him from far away,
He made a crunch when he munched.
He loved it when he found a slimy sock.
Hungry Harry was a snotty boy.
So don't be worried, just stay away.

Dolina Brannan (9)
St Patrick's Primary School, Kilsyth

Roaring Red

Red is a monster who hides
In the shadows, never to be seen.
Definitely not a human being.
He goes house to house every night to see
If he can give someone a fright.
He has glowing red eyes,
Fangs the size of pencils.
Claws as sharp as knives.
So watch out or you'll be next.

John Jack Dynan (10)
St Patrick's Primary School, Kilsyth

Snake Boy

S limy, scaly monster.
N ever ever friendly.
A lways food in his belly.
K eeping food to himself.
E very day he hunts.

B eware, he could be near.
O n the mountains he slays.
Y ou could be next!

Taylor David Burns (10)
St Patrick's Primary School, Kilsyth

My Best Friend Eclipse

Eclipse is a magical monster,
Stars follow her at night
Under the moonlight.
Her fangs are as sharp as her horns,
Her eyes look like an eclipse.
She smells like fish and chips.
Eclipse is a magical poetry monster
And is my best friend forever!

Sophie Boyle (10)
St Patrick's Primary School, Kilsyth

Five Things My Monster Eats

My monster eats dirty socks and soggy pants.
Sometimes he eats mice, and nothing nice.
He eats brains of mice, but I just hope it's not mine!
He likes to eat dogs, as well as frogs.
He likes to eat his own fluff and all other stuff.

Lewis Campbell (9)
St Patrick's Primary School, Kilsyth

Monster

M y monster's name is Joe.
O h no! He's coming.
N ow it's time to hide.
S tomping up the stairs.
T errifying monster.
E ating all the sweets.
R un away and hide.

Kyle Johnston (9)
St Patrick's Primary School, Kilsyth

Shreck

S hreck pokes his head out to see if I'm asleep.
H e can't fit under my bed.
R uns so fast!
E ats too many buns!
C racking his fingers.
K ing of my room.

Thomas Neil (9)
St Patrick's Primary School, Kilsyth

Slimy Monster

I can hear whisperings of anger.
I can smell cotton sheets on his spot.
I can feel the bed moving.
I can taste hunger in the air.
I can feel slimy goo.
I can taste pickles and cheese.
I can feel his slimy body.
I can hear the floor moving.
I can smell yucky slime.

Ella-Louise Whiteley (8)
The Learning Zone, Longfleet Road

Juuj

I could hear his high-pitched growl,
I pretended to sleep and lay down.
I could smell him, he smelt like snot,
I came out of my bed and I dropped.
He stood in front of me,
And called Juuj.

Alex Carlos (10)
The Learning Zone, Longfleet Road

Lola

I can hear the floor creaking.
I can smell red roses.
I can feel her fluffy fur moving around.
I can see Lola eating Mum's wedding cake.
I can taste strawberry icing.

Alice Lloyd (6)
The Learning Zone, Longfleet Road

YOUNG WRITERS INFORMATION

We hope you have enjoyed reading this book – and that you will continue to in the coming years.

If you're a young writer who enjoys reading and creative writing, or the parent of an enthusiastic poet or story writer, do visit our website **www.youngwriters.co.uk**. Here you will find free competitions, workshops and games, as well as recommended reads, a poetry glossary and our blog. There's lots to keep budding writers motivated to write!

If you would like to order further copies of this book, or any of our other titles, then please give us a call or order via your online account.

Young Writers
Remus House
Coltsfoot Drive
Peterborough
PE2 9BF
(01733) 890066
info@youngwriters.co.uk

Join in the conversation!
Tips, news, giveaways and much more!

 YoungWritersUK    @YoungWritersCW